Petition

Books by Joyce Peseroff

Poetry

The Hardness Scale
A Dog in the Lifeboat
Mortal Education
Eastern Mountain Time
Know Thyself
Petition

Edited by Joyce Peseroff

Robert Bly: When Sleepers Awake
The Ploughshares Poetry Reader
Simply Lasting: Writers on Jane Kenyon

Petition

Joyce Peseroff

Carnegie Mellon University Press
Pittsburgh 2020

Acknowledgments

The author is grateful to the editors of the journals and anthologies in which some of the poems in this book first appeared, sometimes in slightly different versions.

Agni Online: "Egg"
American Journal of Poetry: "Cuckoo," "On Choosing One's Manner of Death," "No Signal," "Petition," "Heriz"
Art & Letters: "Dog Tag," "Ghost Story," "The Hidden Life of Trees," "Receipt"
Consequence: "Not Far," "Poem for Young Men Registered as Unaccompanied Minors Seeking Asylum, October 2015"
Ibbetson Street: "Indifference"
Massachusetts Review: "Irish Music"
Memorious: "Dear Thirst"
New Ohio Review: "Horse on a Plane"
On the Seawall: "The Astronauts," "Gathered at the Well"
Open: Journal of Arts & Letters: "Thaw"
Plume: "The High Trees," "La Casa Bellina," "Life on Enceladus"
Salamander: "'Missing Hiker Kept Journal of Her Ordeal'"
The Woven Tale Press: "After a Visit," "Boot Found on the Side of the Road," "Ending with the Corpse Pose"

"After Horace" appeared in *Plume Anthology 5*.
"HitchBOT" was a 2016 Massachusetts Poem of the Moment.
"Lonely in Japan" appeared in *Plume Anthology 7*.
"Poem Beginning with Facebook Meme" was published as a broadside by the Alliance for the Arts, Fort Myers, Florida.
"Poem Beginning with Items from the Vienna Museum of Contraception and Abortion" appeared in *Women of Resistance: Poems for a New Feminism*.
"Springtime Sleep" appeared in the 2018 Alliance for the Arts Chapbook.

With gratitude to my first readers Teresa Cader and Steven Cramer, who helped immeasurably from comma to stanza to section to poem, and finally, to book.

Book design by Miranda Liu

Library of Congress Control Number 2020943664
ISBN 978-0-88748-661-6
Copyright © 2020 by Joyce Peseroff

10   9   8   7   6   5   4   3   2   1

for Jeff and Liz

Contents

I.

II.

III.

I.

Petition

Give the wealth back to those we stole it from.
Give the land back to those we stole it from.

Give our shotguns to those we took the land from.
Maybe they'll split the barrels into irrigation pipes,

maybe they'll mill the stocks for bookends
for the books by those we took language from.

Give love back to those we banished from our love.
Give life back to all who lost insurance for their meds.

Give medicine back to those who find it in a tea,
a weed, a willow, the heat and light in hands

kneading a muscle. Give muscle to the tongue's
back talk, curses, and its sweetest nothings,

the lay of a ripe peach. Give ripeness to a time.
Give us time to restore the forests and the sea

we filtered of whales, codfish, and pink dolphins.
Give us eternity again, we'll set things right.

Not Far

from my front porch, near a bank of the Concord River,
cattails bent and muddy stones slick in December,
is a cell, many cells, where men never see the sun.

And further, far from the hum of my new furnace, is a furnace
lit and relit by a warplane's vector, the pilot burning to powder
city blocks, houses wall to wall, the mother and father inside

churned like concrete, or blasted with shrapnel if they leave,
or by a smoothed-cheeked soldier with an assault rifle.
Light-headed with hunger, they fall under the treads of a tank.

Closer, a man sleeps in a shed with rats, holes in his sleeping bag
shedding feathers. Also a man in a tent, knife at the ready. He hears
the flow of the river stilled by frost that creeps from stones

to the channel, thickening until the passage closes. Air glistens
with snow that shrouds his tiny dwelling. No one would know
that under the mound he is breathing, not his sister, nephew,

stepbrother, those he lied to and stole from, cursed and punched out.
Far from his scabby mittened hands, a boy jaywalks across a street,
bragging to a girl on his phone, shaking a box of candy

for the last piece. He's being followed, maybe by police, maybe
by MS-13. He won't make it to the next block, see the sun again,
or a river, or his grandma's blue mobile home with a saint in the yard

far from Manhattan where lights blink red but no one stops.
A tenant hammering the tower's gilded door is admitted
through the poor door. Past the atrium, rats chase rats upstairs.

"For the Stranger Is Not Foreign, She Is Random"

—Toni Morrison, *The Origin of Others*

Everything I know tells me to retreat
from this woman on the bench
in front of the nail spa asking
if I'll take her home.
She's in pants and long knit sleeves
though it's 90 degrees.
While I brought shirts
to the dry cleaner next door
she was pacing, talking—no cell phone
or Bluetooth. Now she calls
to me. Will I drive her to Lexington—
instead of ripping husks
from sweet corn at Whole Foods.
Her gray hair's trimmed, neat.
She may be younger than me.
It's hot. She has no purse.
Wrong to call the police, agreed.
I could offer to pay for a cab.
"Feed my sheep," the gospel choirs.
"Don't talk to strangers,"
Mom warned me and I warned Liz.
What could this anxious
beggar do I couldn't undo? Timid,
Jeff calls my driving,
as if to summarize my life.

The Astronauts

If I'm the sun, then people I love
whirl past me in elliptical orbits
like comets, once in a hundred years.
And if I'm a planet, each is a moon
with a dark side. Crooked in the arm
of a galaxy, I spiral at light speed,
but since all matter's in motion I
appear to be sitting still
in an armchair, reading the learned
astronomer's biography. Cecilia
Payne-Gaposchkin, who charted
more stars than anyone in her Harvard
observatory, lived down the street
from where my daughter fought
first to root then to be free
of Daddy and me. Astronauts,
argonauts, kids want to be naught
but themselves, without our gravity
warping the space and time a hero
claims. Snubbing the likeness of all
happy families, they're eager to grapple
with Venus and Mars, or the Martian
twin satellites, Terror and Fear. I siren
come closer, darlings—both are here.

Receipt

The cashier at CVS asks if I want a receipt and I smile no.

The gas pump screen chimes RECEIPT YES/NO and I tap NO since I heard the ink on the paper is carcinogenic. Or maybe the paper itself.

Buying groceries I crumple a two-foot printout I don't need since every transaction's recorded by my credit card and I don't bother with coupons.

No one questions whether I own my lunch meat, or prescription, or the fuel that guns me out of town.

I overheard a man laugh in Sears when asked if he wanted a bag for his Gold Toes, "Are you kidding? A Black man walking out of here with pair of socks in his hand?"

Whereas I disdain plastic bags that might stuff a landfill.

Whereas no one will ask whether I own the shoes I wear leaving the store, my old sandals left in a box for the clerk to dispose of.

In three towns in three states no one looks twice when I drop something into my purse. Could be nail polish, could be a gun, could be a bottle I'm nipping at.

Hello, #whiteladyfeminist who never got a ticket, always a warning, OK'd for TSA PreCheck.

If I want to return a sweater, I'll return the sweater, with or without a receipt.

No Signal

I listened, as I drove, to a program on regret—
the good kind that teaches you
to grab the French horn medley
you once thought you'd fuck up,

and the bad, as when a friend dies
without your call or note
and for years you're certain a word
would've shoved his pills back in the bottle.

I regretted most the decades wasted
evading my mother—now I sound like her,
color my hair, catch her eye in the mirror.
Too late to golf with my father.

Static whispered between mountains.
When the signal returned, a woman from Ghana,
London and Philly disemboweled the questions,
"What are you? Where are you from?"

I recalled a Garden Club trainee
passing me as I waited for my hostess
in her kitchen—was this Black woman
joining us for bridge? The trainee

must have seen my look. Meaning,
you're less than human. Meaning,
you're not powerful like us. More
static as the dashboard read NO SIGNAL.

The Hidden Life of Trees

Trees want to be tight,
dense forests, I read in a book
manufactured from their bodies.
A seedling planted solo
suffers like a prisoner locked

in solitary, while the forest's
a gang sharing candy
and muscle. A stump can live
300 years if its fellow Bloods
chip in on life support, roots
connecting like electric cords.

Once I paid to plant a tree
in memory of my grandfather,
one of the murdered, and to make
the desert bloom. What blooms
in a desert? Murder,

as con men on the hilly, arid site
uproot one group of saplings
so another day's busload
of the bereaved will have
some spadework to do.

Jury Duty

Langston Hughes
threw all his books
into the Atlantic Ocean—
textbooks from Columbia,
novels, poems.
He decided to read
people instead. Another
writer jumped ship
when he saw a fellow-
sailor wanted to kill him:
there's always a way
to die on a boat. Now
I've appropriated two
stories from two men,
one Black, one white.
I could say I've boxed
a hundred books
for the dumpster,
or escaped from the car
of a possible rapist—
the Porsche still moving—
and saw him on campus
a number of times.
Time numbs, or doesn't.
Sitting in a jury room
ready to be excused
or sworn, I study the fact of
so much depends. One word
against another, a record
in black and white we
the people transcribe—

if we're not dismissed,
which is what the woman
I read reading beside me
hopes and desires.

Dog Tag

In second grade I was issued a steel dog tag stamped with my name and address.

Then if the Russians bombed PS 89, our parents could find us in hospitals or bury us.

I liked to roll the beaded silver chain between forefinger and thumb.

Dropping the last bead into a diamond-shaped hole in the clasp, I'd pull and the bead vanished. Over and over my fingernail popped it out again.

What kind of country gives its children dog tags? The same that lined us up in the lunchroom for polio shots, classmates screaming behind a screen.

A-bomb, H-bomb, sterilization by mumps—old terrors, succeeded by new.

A popular debate: with hands on the nuclear clock about to clap at midnight, reproduce or not?

We who waited for yes now wait for grandchildren.

Maybe the war will end before Jin and Ottessa can enlist.

Maybe cops will pull daffodils from holsters, and no one study to shoot up a kindergarten.

Pray Shaquille and Padma scrub the air of arsenic, filter lakes florid
with algae, drive electric cars.

Hope their young, lobes diamond-studded with tracking chips,
choose Planet A.

Nullification

In a Facebook video, a bird flies at the feet of a man lifting fresh spadefuls of earth.

The bird picks through each clod for a spasm of white worms, a breed that sucks the gardener's flowers dry.

He turns the soil, edging his spade to guide the bird to the worms, the bird dipping its head.

I know a farmer in Maine who used a chicken tractor to clear his acre of pests, the chickens in a bottomless wire cage rolled from one parcel to the next.

At night I stream a movie about O. J. Simpson. In the back seat of his Bronco, the Juice presses a gun barrel to his head.

Back then Liz was in fourth grade, F. Lee Bailey's ex-wife was her teacher.

I worked full time, and friends obsessed with the trial confused me. Who doubts the guilt of a man caught beating his wife?

I'd seen the Rodney King video and, later, trash cans spinning through windows, fires bulging. Heard the clap of gunshots, grieving sirens.

Who can't guess why a man wouldn't offer his wrists to the police? A rich Black man divorced from a white woman.

The Metco student we hosted visited Thursday afternoons. Her mom sat her on a bus in Boston MTuWThF at 6:00 a.m., waited for her at 5:00 p.m.

Sometimes the bus ran late, Ashleigh sleeping past her stop.

The one Kardashian who wouldn't make a cent from his name is dead; Johnnie Cochran too. O. J. Simpson, paroled from a Nevada prison, will never get his trophies back.

In the movie, the trial of the century lasts nine months, long enough to have a baby. Not guilty, the jury longs to decide.

Their answer to whether we can all get along is no.

Gathered at the Well

Your land was taken from you:
the definition of history
for those with land to take.
I'm a stray myself, sometimes
welcome, often cursed, whether
I had gold or not. I was taught
to remember exile
from air I never breathed.
From what, I understood:
not mine, the olive grove.
Not mine, a net thrashing with fish.
No place in the ceremony,
no bride-price or dowry
for my tongue-tied children.
I suppose my ancestors once
had land, and it was taken,
perhaps by your ancestors.
Now we're both wanderers:
if one of us steals, others
swear we're all thieves.
You recognize the fragrance
of what you lost and of things
likely to be lost. I know the narrow
pass from here to tomorrow
where everyone's a stranger,
all those gathered at the well
arguing my right to drink.
Day by day I carry a house
on my back, in thunder
or a blizzard, on starless nights:
to you, I'm also a stranger.

I ask, where is the road?
When you point south,
I think I should go north.

Poem for Young Men Registered as Unaccompanied Minors Seeking Asylum, October 2015

Like thoroughbreds, they're all given
the same birthday, and like yesterday's
frisking colts they don't know why
they were born to run far and fast,
tracked to the edge of the world
without brother or sister, into a trailer,
onto a ship, locked up and cross-tied.
Imported, stalled, left in the dark,
a horse nickers and lowers his muzzle
to the makeshift rope halter, walks
through a broken fence, and stands
for the knife two men twist in his ribs.
The young girl who finds the body
minus its front legs, haunches filleted,
shakes the air with screams, bugling
her panic as loud as a bachelor band
of boys claiming to be seventeen,
not men of eighteen unprotected by
law or covenant. No child can unsee
what he's seen. They sit in barracks
learning German. When they call
Mama, no one answers. Her cell phone's
lost; the battery died; she's on her way.

HitchBOT

> After traveling across Canada, the Netherlands, and
> Germany, HitchBOT, the hitchhiking robot, gets beheaded
> in Philadelphia.
>   —CNN, August 4, 2015

HitchBOT, you look like a toy in a war zone,
a photograph staged
to crack the heart.

HitchBOT, you're like my kid's old Barbie,
dressed and undressed, decapitated
with familiar contempt.

HitchBOT, you're the highway's first
dweeby victim in a horror movie
franchise, Son or Revenge Of.

Spare battery in a suitcase, suitcase
Velcroed to foam noodle arms
by helpful Canadians,

Germans, or Dutch—gone with your flag,
goofy recital of local trivia,
your emoji face.

You offered the chance for a quick selfie
in the voice of a woman
or prepubescent boy

excited to tour the Grand Canyon. Maybe
that voice enraged some guy
whose job was going

the way of the travel agent, file clerk,
or trucker in a future
of self-driving cars.

Sorry the open road didn't work
for you—that's true for
migrating humans too.

Egg

Who imagines the future as it will happen.

Did Mandelstam think he'd die for comparing Stalin's fingers to grubs.

The night of his arrest, his wife invited Akhmatova for dinner and boiled her an egg.

A fresh egg was a rare thing.

Before the secret police took him, Mandelstam ate the egg Akhmatova offered with salt.

I clean the refrigerator before leaving the place I've lived for six months.

There's a carton with one egg left.

The look of hibiscus beguiled me, and jasmine perfume, for half a year.

I cared for now, forget the future.

Now what should I do with this egg.

Not enough for a meal, stale, maybe good for a batch of pancakes.

My mother said wasting food is a sin.

There are people on this planet, thousands, who'd die for an egg.

Though at my age it won't, I assume the future will be like now.

My friends would laugh if I gave them a single egg.

Would my mother laugh, or her mother, widowed with three children.

I drop the egg.

The disposal grinds it to a slurry that will be flushed and purified, mingled with the river and salting the sea.

This is my lyric for failing to find one of the homeless vets camped by the river and giving him the egg.

I kayaked once past a tent patched with a blue tarp and Jeff, curious, wanted to paddle ashore.

I could barely find breath to say No, so profound was the privacy of a sandy crescent between mangroves.

A tent, a hibachi, a folding chair, a Styrofoam cooler—who could have dreamed this future.

And an egg, what could one egg do to redeem it.

II.

The High Trees

for Donald Hall, 1928-2018

White farmhouse with its porch, clapboard ell, and shingled barn
I'll never see again. The maple in the center of the circular drive

cut down, century-old bushes chainsawed with the barn jacked up,
men and women who sniffed roses in spring and called them pretty

I'll miss always. White church with a simple altar cloth, doors
just wide enough for the casket and trembling men who carry it,

goodbye. The quaint inn, the college town with clever names for
    shops and bars,
no reason to return. From Rt. 4 to 104 past the Bristol Five and
    Dime reopened

as a jumble shop—so like the Bristol Five and Dime—past
    whirligigs
once wood, now plastic, spruce hills on either side steep in
    summer's

long low light, goodbye. Goodbye to Ragged Mountain where I
    planned
to ski but never did, stopping by the farmhouse after lifts closed,
    enough

time for wine and Brie before driving home. Blackwater Dam,
    Newfound Lake,
acres of sweet corn planted in succession so none go without, even
    for a week—

hayfield, hayfield, hayfield, a cemetery called Homeland, tiny
    airport on

Winnipesaukee's shore, outboards rooster-tailing it across the bay.
No more
worry over what I'd missed in conversation, or two layers of
sweatpants
in July. The granite stone bulked three times larger in my memory,
twenty years

since we last stood astonished, red-faced, terrified, bitter, howling
or silent.
Jane's brother pointed, look how high the trees above their grave
have grown.

"Missing Hiker Kept Journal of Her Ordeal"

—The Boston Globe, May 26, 2016

Abandon the path just once, if only to pee, and you're lost.

First text, undelivered—"Im in somm trouble.
Call AMC. Somewhere north of woods road"—

When I missed a blue marker the hour before sunset, I wasn't
afraid. Our land, after all. At worst, I could about-face and follow
the waddle my snowshoes tracked.

Next day—"Off trail 3 or 4 mi. Call police"—texted to her
husband, never received.

But I kept searching. Air whisked between fleece and skin. I began
to sweat.

In the woods, Pan rules. Follow his pipes and wander in circles.

Two days later, when she missed an off-trail meet-up, wardens
stamped through the brush blowing emergency whistles, calling her
name.

Can I understand the pain of others only by suffering, which I
hate?

After three weeks in her sleeping bag—dull with starvation,
exposure—I know she knew she was dying.

Or is suffering a thicket with a bird inside, every other singer
competition for a mate?

Clouds covered the sun. Ice pellets flung by my ski pole rolled and scribbled as they slid down a drift. An oak rattled three leaves on a single stem.

"When you find my body, please call"— discovered on a Navy training base.

Sun dropped below the clouds. A silver arrow glinted from a blue marker—lower on the oak than I expected, three feet of snow girdling its trunk.

A moment of terror. Ten minutes. Nothing, but something. Nothing. Something.

—"my husband George and my daughter Kerry"—notebook removed two years later, two miles west of the trail, inside her blue tent.

Photo of items placed outside the tent: a bandana, rosary, birthday candles, lighter, dental floss, a sewing kit, and two plastic water bottles, one half full.

Ghost Story

A ghost is neither here nor there.

A ghost is trapped

like the image between white scalloped

borders in a snapshot friends gave me

of my husband kissing another woman

five years before we met.

They're both so young—

Jeff with his long hair,

his girlfriend in a twin set.

Crowded on the bed in a basement

student apartment, aren't they

the very spirit of love?

If Jeff should gaze

once more into her unlined face,

he might yearn like the character

who senses her lover's ghost in a tune

sung at a Christmas party.

Suddenly her husband

understands their marriage—

as dead as the boy whose voice

his wife hasn't heard for twenty years.

And what happens after I die?

A widower reheats beef stew

and he's ready to live serenely

exchanging the gift of his life

with a woman who ferments

her own cabbage and beer.

After a Visit

A kiss at the airport—

You satisfied to leave

Me driving in the dark

With one headlight.

Thaw

Twenty days of twenty below drove frost deep into the ground.

Its rage at being buried alive throws stones, cracks blacktop.

By day freshets of snowmelt surge through the woodshed.

At night they freeze our front door shut.

The kitchen sink won't drain: the pipe's a handhold for climbing ice.

I boil and pour kettle after kettle, open an artery to spring's cold heart.

Each frozen crystal requires a nucleus, particle bound to a lattice as rigid as copper.

Let's let the nub of our bitterness go.

Around us, winter's dissolving.

The road is mud, but it's still a road.

Snowbird Song

In March I google words
that will startle local Book Club
women out of their bodies
into tufts of moss, ferns unfurling,

sedges grown inch by inch,
the sparrow's Peabody, Peabody—
a New England spring as far
from the Gulf as apples

from oranges. I left my volumes—
Dickinson, Williams, Rich—
in Massachusetts with you,
another faraway love I touch
through wireless ether, listen to

but can't inhale like earth
after soaking, equinoctial rain.
I haven't seen a crocus burst
its button from lacy snow,
or forsythia bloom, or peepers

pipe their lust in four winterless
years. Tonight, waiting for
my return, you hold your phone
out the car window so I can hear.

Lonely in Japan

In Japan, you can hire a family if your wife has died and your daughter won't speak to you.

You fill a form with their common gestures and favorite foods. Nicknames and hairstyles.

Nights are loneliest, the blue face of the TV evident to revelers and dog walkers.

Nights when you don't speak to a soul except yourself, talking to yourself a habit.

Some think America's the loneliest place, miles between towns, neighbors you avoid because they own guns.

An old Japanese woman raises her window shade each morning, watching the old woman across the courtyard raise her shade, expecting she will notice the day it stays down.

But she forgets which window she's checking, and whether someone new has moved into the other apartment.

Some nights I watch the sun drop, the clouds go plum. A loud splash from the pond, a susurrus of crickets, what whistles like a whip-poor-will.

None of these voices comforts me.

Would I hire comfort, and what's the difference between a comforter and a friend?

Job's comforters made things worse.

Left without cattle, house and barn burned, children slaughtered, Job's wife said, "Curse God and die."

Loneliness says the same.

Maybe I'll hire a small god who washes my feet with water sprayed from his trunk.

Out of our bodies we'd sail, over the Peace River, trumpeting our blessed detachment above the black mangroves whose salty leaves taste like tears.

Admit there are more transistors in the world than leaves on trees.

Admit this adds to the world's loneliness as seen from the back of a small god, rented for a few hours like a hotel room in a city where your visa has expired.

In a foreign capital with a population of one, there's still hope that one will be your friend.

Indifference

I want to bake beans in July's
narrow kitchen, though
the poorly insulated oven's
in bad enough repair
to fry the entire house.

The opposite of life? Indifference.
Ditto, the opposite of love.
Generations ignored the bump
of rain on a rusty roof,
shingles crackled, paint loose,

and a mouse nest made of pink
fiberglass behind the stove's
enamel door. Days of steel-
wool passion, Skunk-Off,
and the dial set to Broil

scoured away the smell.
Now I'm washing curtains,
preparing for love's arrival—
whoever that may be, vowing I'm ready
to change my life—if I can stand it.

La Casa Bellina

You seemed happy,
said you were in love—
someone completely unsuitable,
oh, but adorable, sexy, devoted.
Hair trimmed, eyes wide, flush
with wine, joking, gossiping
about friends you'd shown

no interest in a month ago,
you agreed you were better,
if not healed. Dipping fish
into sauce, you improvised for a toddler
the tale of rascal mare Bellina
pinching her rider's hat to spin it
over the moon; you looked happy.

It didn't last. I held your hand
in coffee shops; chain-smoking,
you paced the parking garage.
I panicked you might throw yourself
from a bridge, under a car—
we both knew men who'd done that.

Pills helped. You moved the most
painful photos; new books and CDs
slumped around your chair.
You clipped an ad for L.L. Bean's
"Bi-Polar" jacket. No dividing
contentment now from chemistry
and, dear, I don't know my way

out of this poem. Why
I love a friend or chose to marry
one man, not another—anyone's
guess is as good as mine if "mind"
is merely noise from a molecule's
calibrated blips. Let's walk
past the river. Don't look down—

at the marble step, push open
the door to La Casa Bellina.
We'll swipe bread from the tables, sip
nectar distilled from honey and fog
and stiff the old libation bearers—
naked under black tuxedoes—
throwing silver as we go.

Sonnet on the Solstice

Freakishly warm for December. A fly
abrades its wing against the window frame.
A car as lethal as a gun wounds 35, kills 1.
In my rage, I've pictured darlings dead,
a hard heart simplifying life. Stone soup
simple. Shoots rise a quarter inch—tulips maybe,
can't recall, but what a mistake. By four,
the sun hunkers, the fly a grackle on my nerves.
A twentysomething bastes organic chicken
for her mom, a terminal patient. Other moms
grieve for a prodigal who won't come home.
Overwhelmed by love's bright light, who sees
a thing? My loves, I couldn't bear the dark
without your veined and noisy black lace wings.

Horse on a Plane

A horse on a plane is a dangerous thing
if the box he's persuaded to enter shifts
like a boulder or a coffin fragrant with hay
but no exit and midflight he decides no way,
time to bomb this pop stand, burst out
of his lofty corral into a tufted field
asway with timothy, feathers and prance.
You ask a horse—you don't tell him—to trot
or whoa, easy there fella, and cross-tie him
with a knot meant to fail if he pulls back.
When the plane bucks, a horse can launch
steel shoes through aluminum, the hiss
of oxygen dropping down the masks.
Then his groom must place a pistol barrel
in the nearest ear and whisper, Easy—
carried on with apples, sugar, and oats,
the gun follows the horse on every flight.

On Choosing One's Manner of Death

Time is short.
After reading a few
sonnets detailing American
executions—a slave who poisoned
her master burned alive,
a sailor who insisted
on tying his own noose—

the poet was asked:
if she were condemned,
what method would she pick?
The quickest, she said.
In Utah they hold you down
for a shot through the heart.
Hanging, if the knot's

done right, the rope taut,
and weight accounted for,
is also fast. I thought of
the story—or is it a joke?—
of the wise man captured
by the Great Khan, who then
commanded him to choose

his manner of death. Old age,
the sage replied, and so
gained his lord's protection
for as many years
as the Khan evaded plague,
axe, venom, flame,
and his clever sons.

Poem Beginning with Items from the Vienna Museum of Contraception and Abortion

Rat poison.
A forty-pound rock.
Bundles of herbs.
A grapevine stalk.

Wire clothes hangers.
A scalding bath.
Did you tumble down
stairs or a granite cliff?

A forty-year sentence
in El Salvador.
Three felonies charged
in a Tennessee court.

Go to another state.
Hope for another world
after they bounce you
from this one, girl.

Coins for the Boatman

Maybe you'll moor near leukemia's pod,
the nurse in a hazmat suit peppy and brisk.

Or dare demented me to crush
pills into 8 oz of scotch.

Spare me a March stroked out in the ICU
followed by years on a vent farm.

Let me cheer with a crowd the runners on Boylston St.
or the lead singer canting a hip as the audience
sloshes her way like a spring tide.

Not likely the news will pronounce me
suicide by cop.

To the freezing, blood flows so hot
they throw off their woolly clothes.

Those without carbon monoxide sensors exhale
in bed with no mark of struggle. "I want to die
at home," Jane told Don—leukemia again, sorry.

Like Jane, I'll miss the hermit thrush's arpeggios;
like Don, my friends' poetry.

What I'll feel for Jeff and Liz, I'm glad
I won't have a body to feel.

Raft, barge, yacht, megaship with ten thousand
guests and a crew of one—your prow divides
a silty sea.

Like flying south to my dad in hospice,
I'll pay for a seat to where I don't want to go.

Visiting My Parents' Grave

I know they're not here,
but they chose this place

as they did their condo,
and how wrong not to visit

as I did the white leather
sectional and plasma

TV they denied themselves
until years understood

to be their last. Pink marble
lies flush with spikes

of Bermuda grass so the mower
will find no impediment,

and there's no leaving
the traditional pebble

beside the epitaph my mother
inscribed for them both:

Forever in Our Hearts.
Another mourner's tree

has leapt from the ground
to shade her words, and many

plots behind them fill—
each time I need a map

to the narrow, perpetually
cared-for ground. My Aunt

Rita, who drove, leaves me
alone for five minutes to—

what, pray? I let her throttle
past the gates of Eternal Light,

clutching my seat belt
as she cuts across lanes

of traffic—she can't get out
of the cemetery fast enough.

III.

Dear Thirst

Water came before thirst,
before sand, the sea,
before the tides, the moon,
and sun before Earth.

Bodies lived before love,
and tender leaves before
the hungry ate—raw food
before the age of fire.

Death came seconds after
life, but some life won't die—
a colony of seagrass older
than the marsh that roots it,

a fungus in Oregon larger
than a blue whale. Fish
drown in oil, seeds mutate,
a bird falls from acid skies—

the soul needs a soul-
making vale, the lion a grass-
fed lamb. Dear thirst,
dear life, dear lack—before

desire, the planet was no
gorgeous world, Eden
no poem, the tale no Troy,
Helen a girl herding goats.

After Horace

Ode, Book 4, line 12, "Already the Winds of Thrace . . ."

Now heat opens the supple buds
and warms the shore, gentling winds
that beat the waves to a meringue
of whitecaps, lashing small craft to the docks.

Meadows sprout from oozing mud—
barn swallows patch their nests, dipping
at dusk to pick off gnats like Ms.
Pac Man swallowing pellet-dots.

Horses stretch their necks over the stall door,
scenting the sugary tufts. After an hour's
grazing, a groom pulls them back
to the barn, afraid of new-grass colic.

It's hot! Let's drink. You bring hors d'oeuvres—
a proper cocktail party, not a binge.
Dear friend, it's bad to drink alone—
break out of your cave and sit by me.

Your rich pals moan about missed putts
while you shudder over life and death.
Split a magnum, buy a tin of caviar—
we'll laugh at rogues, set the world to rights,

map constellations with double stars,
ignore our achy knuckles, knees and hips
in a self-medicated dance. The guest bed's
made up, don't think of driving home.

Ending with the Corpse Pose

I flip my hands around,
step left a quarter turn,
spine narrow and tall,
inflexible as a ship's mast.
Music surges in a wave—
Shake your booty. The others
pitch and roll like mermaids.
Move in four directions, leg up,
arms down, forward, right—
which I can't tell from left
without a moment's thought—
all meant to stimulate the old
nervous system. And we're
old, that junk in the trunk
packed like our basements.
Soon we'll *shake shake shake*
stem to stern in a perfect storm
of illness and chemo-brain.
We'll swivel our hips past
towers of newspaper, aisles
between shaped by our bent
shoulders. Roll them forward,
back. Point and flex. Stretch,
breathe, lie down in what
yoga calls the corpse pose.
After dancing like a waterspout
as you did at sixteen, tipsy
on wine coolers, be the flood
tide before a full moon. It's
the moon you want, after all.

Life on Enceladus

It's snowing all the time at the south pole of Enceladus
Which is a moon of Saturn
With the loveliest name
And the brightest object in the solar system
Reflecting 98% of the sun's light
Its surface like the best powder day
So cold no life could multiply
Except the orbit of Enceladus
Around Saturn is elliptical
And squeezes the moon's interior
To liquid and also what's frozen
Underneath the white mantle
So now and then a geyser of salt
Water sprays upward and perhaps
Growing in the water a litter of microbes
As yet undiscovered but possible
Its alien DNA unsullied because capped
Beneath ice and acres of snow deeper
Than Everest is high Enceladus
Like the white canvas of eternity
Stroked by a brush with a single hair

Cuckoo

Trees in a drought
vibrate with thirst,
groaning through hollow
capillaries.
Even if the ear
of wheat in the mill
doesn't suffer,
a reaper wounds
the green stalk,
and a maple spreading
its crown to gather
a neighbor's light
is a predator. One life
depends on another
sentenced to death—
so Simone Weil starved
herself to suicide,
which I find as monstrous
as the beautiful Shakers
singing their hymns,
joining their furniture,
living side by side
as celibate equals—
a kind of suicide—
raising children left
like cuckoos in
their milk-painted nest.
Birds on the lip
of extinction still chirp,
and the last two
Sisters of Sabbathday Lake

joked how many
were needed to change
a light bulb: "None—we wait
for a Brother to do it!"

Heriz

The "investment-quality" Oriental we thought
would rise in value as we crushed it underfoot

like grapes for an old vintage, or hopeless love
that multiplies the more the lover's scorned—

we store in the garage, cleaned and wrapped,
an heirloom waiting for an heir to roll it out.

Antique, hand-knotted, hand-dyed, genuine
Persian, the spice of New England rooms

with butler's table, wingbacks, armoire
and a spool bed where the boy jumping off

called his friend's dad Mister—who wants
any part of it? "Brown furniture," the dealers

call that shit. Rug that wore like steel, absorbed
our dogs' vomit, Liz's poster paint, beer,

soot from the fireplace—I miss its geometric
reds and blues, the border's lopsided gazelle

deliberate in the 10 x 14 weave, imperfection
meant to trick the evil eye. So far evil's

blinked at us, our old house sold not burnt
or bulldozed by a mob. The buyers' girls

walked silently, chin down, through their new
rooms—kids don't want to move. But they must.

A Pair of Limmer Boots

The life that required custom leather
hiking boots is gone, and woolen
cross-country knickers with knee
high socks—clothes that used to fit
for things we no longer do.
I bagged them for Goodwill

but you hid them with books
on beekeeping, a boat hook,
and ham radio—not ready
to that admit that choices narrow,
that we can't recalculate our turns
through the world's dark wood.

You'd sent the shop in Intervale
a tracing of each foot the year
before they stopped taking orders.
The night you crept down the Cog
Railway's trestle, the Great Gulf
of Mt. Washington behind you,

stars bright enough to glint
from your metal lace hooks—
what, on that hike, split before
from after, like maternity smocks
and baby clothes, or the mirrored
dress I wore when we first met?

Springtime Sleep

after Meng Hao-Jan

Sleeping through the spring dawn,
I snub the song of a thousand birds—
and a hubbub of wind and rain clubbing
who knows how many flowers.

Springtime, summer, dull November sleep—
a third of my life a blackout.
If the butterfly's me, and I'm a butterfly,
who remembers our dream?

In winter sleep, heartbeat close to death,
a bear delivers her cubs. Somehow
the nurslings—hairless, blind—
understand they've left the womb.

I'm old, love, but you feel like spring.
Forty of them snoring together
with a song that canters through my birdbrain:
Wild, wild horses couldn't drag me away.

Boot Found on the Side of the Road

Emergency bucket,
vase for a tumbleweed,
did your mate fall in love with a snake
or quit you to roll off
yet another man's bed?
Toe in the stirrup,
heel narrowed to a spur,
you rode at sunset
thinking to rest empty
under a tin roof—
rain tum tumming,
sweet cornbread, beans,
floor beneath the mattress
swept clean of spiders.
Instead you're useless
as a peacock feather,
your diamondback leather
tossed like a stoned
hitchhiker, bent double
with laughter after posing
as the Pit Stop Killer.
Now you miss the kick
of human warmth
the way a well longs for water
or a left-handed woman,
palm on the mirror,
grieves for her twin
absorbed by the womb.

A) Don't Do B) Can't Do C) Won't Do

a) Pick lowbush blueberries, bare knees grinding lichen to lint.

b) Acrobatic sex.

c) Ask Jeff whether it rains, since he won't say. "A little mist," maybe, or, "Just a sprinkle," but never, "Yes, it's raining."

*

a) Drink and drive, though I got loopy after one puff of Dave and Mary's blunt before tasting a chicken gumbo dinner that grew more delicious each minute. They invited me to stay the night but I said, "I'll be fine in half an hour," and I was.

b) Climb Acadia's Precipice Trail as power couples jog over crevices in quick, loping strides. Or cluster to watch one of them, wrapped in an orange tarp, coptered off a ledge.

c) Sleep in blankets on the floor after driving 200 miles for dinner with a man who'd never been my lover.

*

a) Sail when the wind's 25 knots, small craft warnings, spume.

b) Sit on my heels, though Jeff swears with practice I could.

c) Salve my feet, sored like a mule's back after years of missteps, the path behind me vapor.

*

a) Open the bud of my fears. The center makes me quail.

b) Trust in the soul, though the morning Jane died a gray sport of the typically rufous song sparrow convinced me she was quivering through its trill and I shouted, "The spirit is not the body!"

c) Give my location to time's Uber driver, preferring to trudge.

Florida Meme

Here in the state
with the prettiest name
winter nestles its fruit

in plastic clamshells,
and Florida Man
Crashes Car while trying

to time travel. Strawberries
are an impulse buy (redder
doesn't mean sweeter)

and Florida Man,
like a model berry—
Radiant, Winterstar—thrives

in hurricane and drought.
He Walks Alligator
into Liquor Store,

he inspires craft beer
with a hint of citrus
(also Colombian Man

Killed by Flying Toilet,
who tries to convince
authorities he's not dead).

Searches for Florida Man
spiked in summer
2018 while strawberries

peak January-March,
2 quarts/$5 fragrant
as rumor, a rainfall, a laugh.

Poem Beginning with Facebook Meme

There are 500 sheep in this photo.
Can you see them yet? and I can't,
since I assume sheep are white
acres of wool the kids in 4-H
washed and primped, or like a cloud
in a children's book. So I'm fooled
into staring at lumps of snow
in a weedy foreground. Wary
of the photographer, the sheep
stand back in clumps—necks
turned and rumps to the wind—
grayish-brown, like weeds. Outside
the 4-H barn, a calf strapped flat
to a tabletop looked ready to be flayed,
but the knife stopped at each horny
hoof. Feet trimmed, the heifer tilted
back to her feet as two men cranked
her and the tabletop upright.

Turkeys in Twilight

look like Edward Gorey drawings
of widows in dark weeds
bent against the wind, their tails
the blowing vents of winter coats.

But it's summer,
and the widows are marching,
protesting war or pension cuts
or the bridge collapse

that plucked them from their toms.
In truth, they're moms with half-
grown poults—in silhouette
they pass, pecking at grass,

single file, shadows merging
with the phantom lower limbs
of pines. Unlike chickens,
they don't cluster over

a promising tuft, or gabble
approval to one another.
Quiet and austere, into conservation
land the feral disappears.

Irish Music

A blind man with sight
surgically restored
can't recognize what he sees

in blobs of color, puzzle shapes.
He walks in a painting
by Klee or Miró—

with no depth perception,
everything's flat.
To a woman with Alzheimer's

a dark red rug
looks like a hole in the floor—
a bloody hole. She can't open

her front door
without stepping past it
and won't let anyone in

except a blind man maybe
who wouldn't notice anything
amiss. In movies, a doctor

unwraps enough bandages
to succor a regiment
before the big reveal—

the hero can see again!
In life, the newly sighted
sometimes prefer darkness

to looming abstractions
accelerating past
at hard-to-reckon speeds

so the operation is reversed,
which allows the man to sit
next to the demented woman—

a sweet woman, who loves Irish
music—and hold her hand
as long as it needs to be held.

Notes

"For the Stranger Is Not Foreign, She Is Random": <https://blogs.lse.ac.uk/lsereviewofbooks/2018/01/25/book-review-the-origin-of-others-by-toni-morrison/>

"HitchBOT": <https://www.cnn.com/2015/08/03/us/hitchbot-robot-beheaded-philadelphia-feat/index.html>

"'Missing Hiker Kept Journal of Her Ordeal'": <https://www.bostonglobe.com/metro/2016/05/25/hiker-who-died-after-disappearing-from-appalachian-trail-survived-for-weeks/KAcHuKSdYVHNTNu0qQobvK/story.html>

"Snowbird Song" is based on Jane Kenyon's "The Clearing."

"On Choosing One's Manner of Death" is for Jill McDonough and *Habeas Corpus.*